Conductors and Insulators

Chris Oxlade

Raintree

www.raintreepublishers.co.uk
Visit our website to find out more information about Raintree books.

To order:
☎ Phone 0845 6044371
🖷 Fax +44 (0) 1865 312263
🖳 Email myorders@raintreepublishers.co.uk

Customers from outside the UK please telephone +44 1865 312262

Raintree is an imprint of Capstone Global Library Limited, a company incorporated in England and Wales having its registered office at 7 Pilgrim Street, London, EC4V 6LB – Registered company number: 6695582

Edited by Daniel Nunn, Rebecca Rissman, and Catherine Veitch
Designed by Joanna Hinton-Malivoire
Picture research by Elizabeth Alexander
Production by Eirian Griffiths
Originated by Capstone Global Library Ltd
Printed and bound in China by Leo Paper Products Ltd

ISBN 978 1 406 23227 1 (hardback)
15 14 13 12
10 9 8 7 6 5 4 3 2

ISBN 978 1 406 23232 5 (paperback)
16 15 14 13 12
10 9 8 7 6 5 4 3 2 1

British Library Cataloguing in Publication Data
Oxlade, Chris.
Conductors and insulators. -- (It's electric!)
621.3'193-dc22
A full catalogue record for this book is available from the British Library.

Acknowledgements
The author and publisher are grateful to the following for permission to reproduce photographs: Alamy p. 21 (© Paul Glendell); © Capstone Global Library Ltd pp. 9 (Lord and Leverett), 12 (Lord and Leverett), 18 (Lord and Leverett), 19 (Lord and Leverett), 20 (Lord and Leverett); Capstone Publishers pp. 6 (Karon Dubke), 8 (Karon Dubke), 10 (Karon Dubke), 11 (Karon Dubke); iStockphoto p 15 (© Albert Lozano); Photolibrary p. 29 (Corbis InsideOutPix); Shutterstock pp. 4 (© yampi), 5 (© Joshua Haviv), 7 (© eprom), 13 (© Philip Lange), 14 (© ~vvetc~), 16 (© c.), 17 (© Ermes), 22 (© WitR), 23 (© crydo), 26 (© Anettphoto), 27 (© Cedric Weber), 28 (© PLRANG), 24 (© HomeStudio), 25 (© CROM).

Cover photograph of a hand holding different wires reproduced with permission of Shutterstock (© April Cat). Design background feature reproduced with permission of Shutterstock (© echo3005).
The publisher would like to thank Terence Alexander for his assistance in the preparation of this book.

Contents

What is electricity? 4
Electric circuits. 6
Conductors and insulators 8
Testing materials 10
Conductors 12
Using conductors 14
Circuit boards 16
Insulators 18
Insulators for safety 20
Power lines 22
Semiconductors 24
Sparks and lightning 26
Electricity and water 28
Glossary 30
Find out more 31
Index 32

Some words are shown in bold, **like this**.
You can find them in the glossary on page 30.

What is electricity?

How many machines have you used today that work by using electricity? You might have listened to a music player, watched television, played with a **battery**-powered toy, or switched on a light.

How many electric machines can you see here?

Electricity lights up our towns and cities at night.

We use electric machines every day at home, at school, at work, and in factories. They do lots of jobs for us. Imagine trying to live without them!

Electric circuits

In this circuit, the battery pushes electricity through the bulb.

An electric **circuit** is a loop that electricity can flow round. Electricity does not flow around a circuit on its own. It needs a push. In this simple circuit a **battery** makes the push.

A circuit is made up of parts called **components**. The components are connected, or joined, with wires. The electricity flows along the wires and through the components.

wire

component

Components are connected with metal wires to make a circuit.

Conductors and insulators

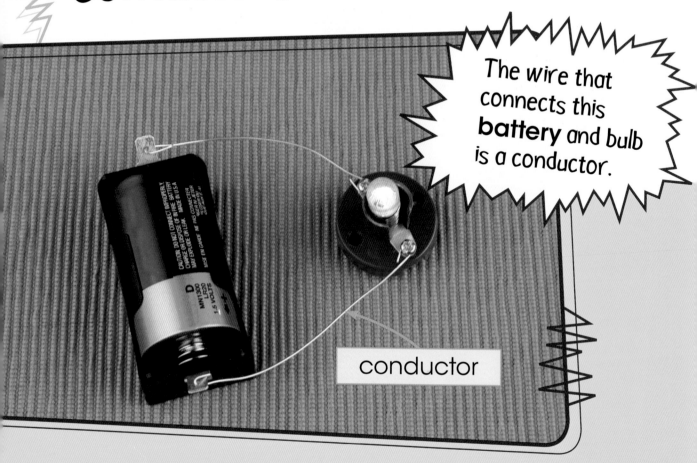

The wire that connects this **battery** and bulb is a conductor.

conductor

Electricity cannot flow everywhere. Materials that electricity can flow through are called **conductors**. We use conductors to make electric **circuits**.

Electricity cannot flow through most materials. We call these materials **insulators**. We cannot make electric circuits from insulators.

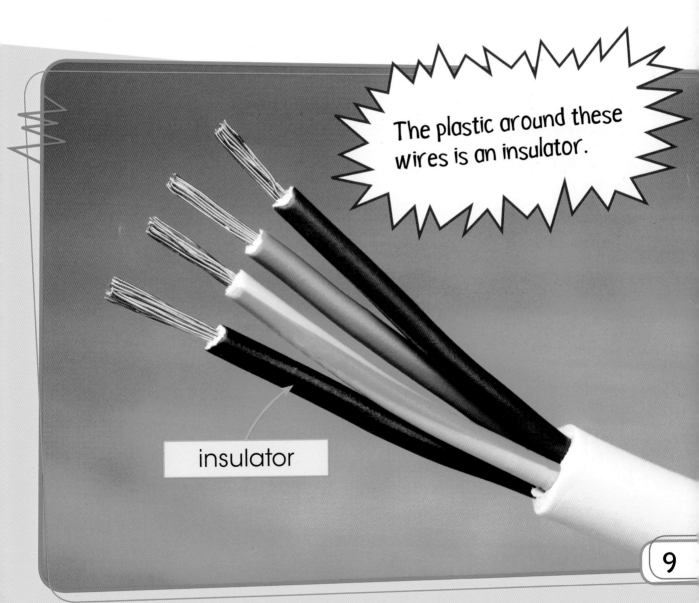

The plastic around these wires is an insulator.

insulator

Testing materials

How do we know if a material is a **conductor** or an **insulator**? We can use a simple test. We can put a piece of the material in an electric **circuit** and see if the circuit works.

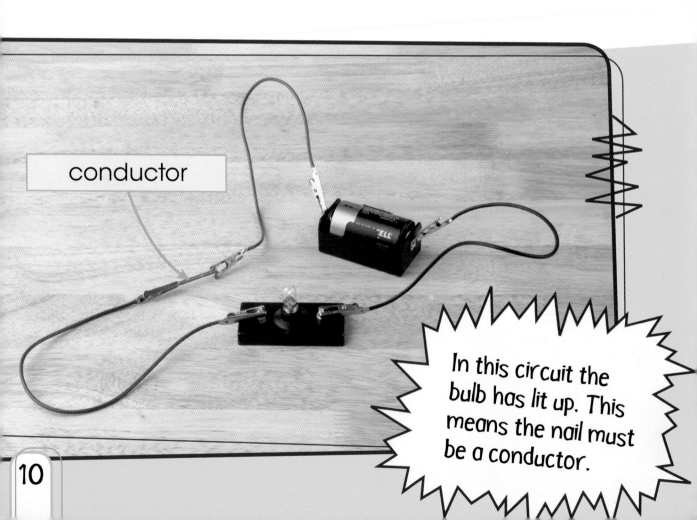

conductor

In this circuit the bulb has lit up. This means the nail must be a conductor.

If the material is a conductor, electricity flows through it and the bulb lights up. If the material is an insulator, electricity cannot flow through it and the bulb does not light up.

insulator

In this circuit the bulb has not lit up. This means the spoon must be an insulator.

Conductors

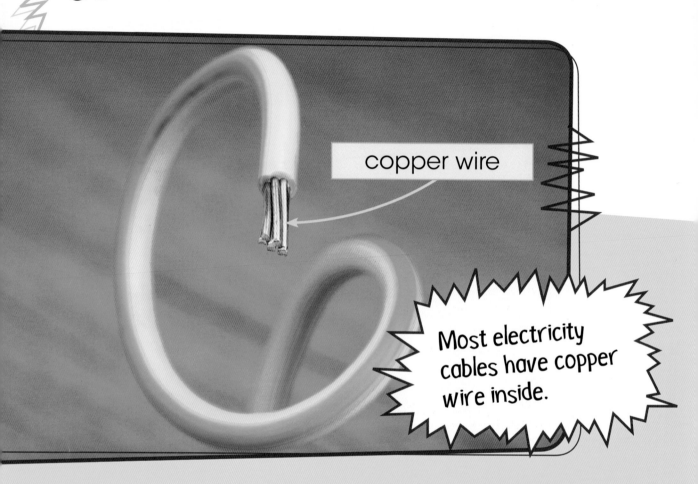

copper wire

Most electricity cables have copper wire inside.

A **conductor** is a material that lets electricity flow through it. Most conductors are metals. Most metals are hard, shiny materials. Copper, steel, iron, **aluminium**, and tin are all conductors.

Gold and silver are metals. They are very good conductors. Electricity flows through them easily. But they are expensive. A conductor that is not a metal is graphite. This is the material in a pencil lead.

Gold and silver are often used in cables for televisions because they let signals pass through clearly.

Using conductors

These cables are part of a computer network.

Anything that works using electricity has **conductors** in it. Cables carry electricity from one place to another. Cables come in many sizes and colours. They all have wire in them that is made of a conductor.

The **components** in **circuits** also contain conductors. There are coils made of copper wire inside an electric motor. When electricity flows through the copper, the coil turns into a magnet, and the motor spins.

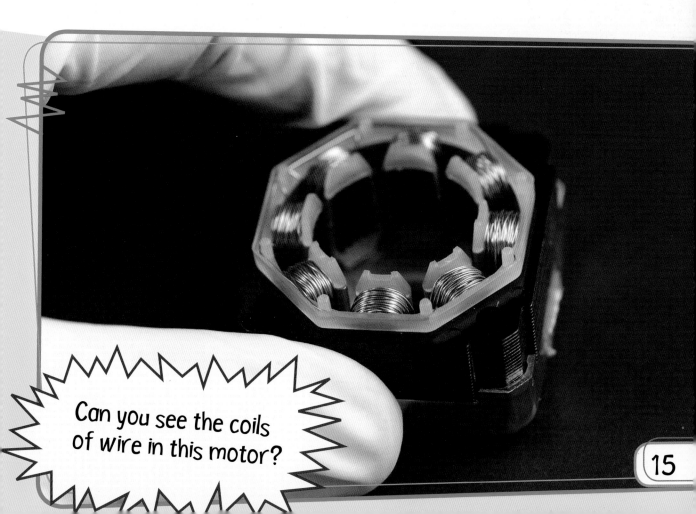

Can you see the coils of wire in this motor?

Circuit boards

track

This circuit board has copper tracks that carry electricity around.

Machines such as televisions and mobile phones contain **circuit boards**. A circuit board is a thin sheet of plastic with **components** attached to it.

Components are attached to a circuit board with a material called **solder**. Solder is a **conductor**. It is made mostly of tin. To make a connection, the solder is melted. It flows around the wires, cools, and then goes hard.

tin

A soldering gun heats and melts the tin.

Insulators

An **insulator** is a material that does not let electricity flow through it. Most materials are insulators. Plastic, rubber, paper, wood, and ceramics are all insulators.

The plastic around wires is known as insulation.

We use insulators to stop electricity flowing where we don't want it. Plastic insulation around wire stops electricity escaping if the wire touches something metal.

Plastic boxes and insulating tape are sometimes used to cover up wires.

Insulators for safety

Plastic insulation covers the wires inside this power cable.

Household electricity is very powerful. It can injure a person, and even kill. So you must never play with electricity sockets or plugs. Cables that carry household electricity are always covered in thick **insulation**.

The electricity in power lines and railway lines is even more powerful than household electricity. That's why you should never play near power lines or on railways.

This man is wearing goggles and special insulated gloves to protect him.

Power lines

Power lines are held up by pylons.

The electricity we use at home is made at electricity generating stations. It gets to our homes along thick cables called power lines. The cables are made of a metal called **aluminium**, which is a **conductor**.

Glass insulators stop electricity flowing to the pylons.

Insulators are very important in power lines. They stop the powerful electricity from escaping. There are insulators made of glass between the power cables and the pylons.

Semiconductors

A semiconductor is a material that conducts electricity but not as strongly as a metal. **Transistors** and **diodes** are made from semiconductors. Transistors and diodes are **components** in a circuit.

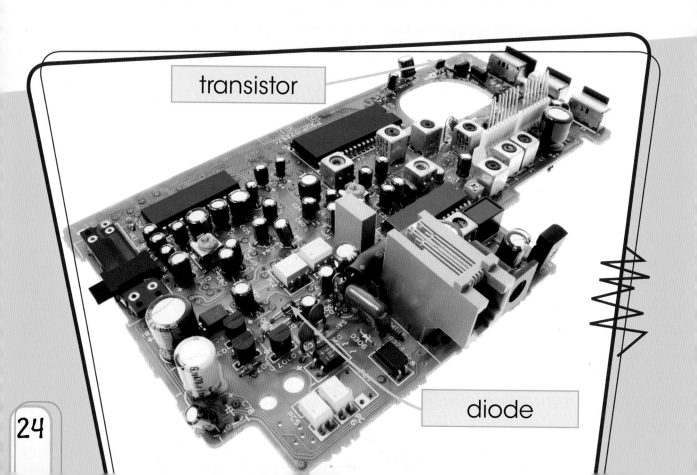

transistor

diode

We use transistors and diodes in computers, mobile telephones, televisions, and other electronic machines. A **microchip** is a piece of semiconductor that has thousands or even millions of transistors on it.

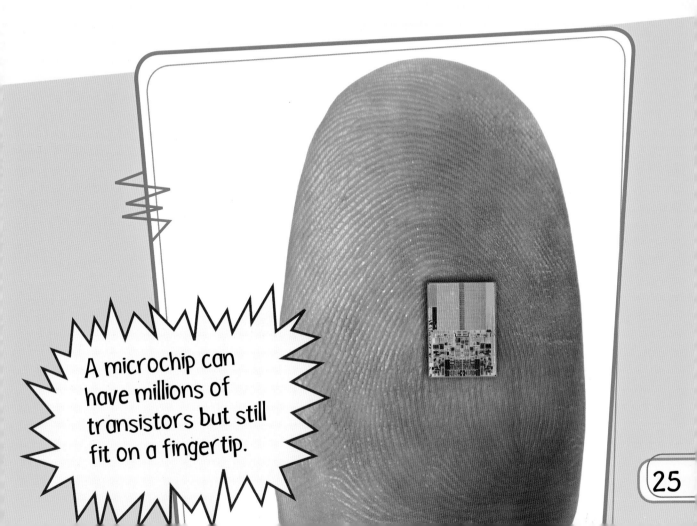

A microchip can have millions of transistors but still fit on a fingertip.

Sparks and lightning

Air is normally an **insulator**. But when you put **batteries** into a toy, you might see tiny sparks. The sparks are made by electricity jumping through the air. A flash of lightning is a giant spark.

Lightning is electricity jumping most often from a cloud to the ground.

Lightning often jumps from clouds to the top of tall buildings. It can damage the buildings and hurt anyone inside. Tall buildings have a lightning **conductor**. A lightning conductor is a thick copper strip that carries electricity from lightning safely to the ground.

lightning conductor

Electricity and water

Outdoor electricity sockets are covered to stop water from getting in.

Water is not a good **conductor** of electricity. But water is not an **insulator** either. Electricity can flow through water. You should always keep water away from electrical things.

A mixture of household electricity and water is very dangerous. If you touch a light switch or wall socket with wet hands, electricity can flow into you. You could be badly hurt.

For safety, never touch a light switch with wet hands.

Glossary

aluminium grey metal that is a conductor

battery part that pushes electricity around a circuit

circuit loop that electricity flows around

circuit board plastic board with parts attached to it

component something that does a job in an electric circuit, such as a battery or a bulb

conductor material that electricity can flow through

diode part in a circuit that is a semiconductor

insulation materials used to stop electricity from escaping

insulator material that electricity cannot flow through

microchip small part that contains a very complicated electric circuit

solder material that is a conductor, used to connect parts

transistor part in a circuit that is a semiconductor

Find out more

Books

Conductors and Insulators (My World of Science), Angela Royston
(Raintree Publishers, 2008)

Electricity (Investigate), Chris Oxlade
(Raintree Publishers, 2008)

The Facts about Electricity, Rebecca Hunter
(Franklin Watts, 2007)

Websites

**www.bbc.co.uk/schools/scienceclips/
ages/6_7/electricity.shtml**
Animated interactive games about electricity
from the BBC.

**www.bbc.co.uk/schools/teachers/
keystage_1/activities/science2.shtml**
Try this quiz from the BBC website.

www.switchedonkids.org.uk/
Lots of electricity activites, games, and puzzles.

Index

batteries 4, 6, 8, 26
bulbs 6, 8, 10, 11

circuit board 16, 17
circuits 6, 7, 8, 9, 10, 11,
    15, 24
components 7, 15,
    16, 17, 24
conductor 8, 10, 11,
    12, 13, 14, 15, 17, 22,
    24, 27, 28

insulating tape 19
insulators 8, 9, 10, 11,
    18, 19, 20, 23, 26, 28

lightning 26, 27
lights 4, 5

metals 12, 13

plugs 20
power lines 21, 22, 23
pylons 22, 23

semiconductor 24, 25
sockets 20, 28, 29
solder 17
switch 29

wires 7, 8, 9, 14, 17, 18,
    19, 20